THE LITTL

BRI

MACHINE TIPS

ANDREW LANGLEY

THE LITTLE BOOK OF BREAD MACHINE TIPS

ANDREW LANGLEY

First published in Great Britain in 2013 by
Absolute Press, an imprint of Bloomsbury Publishing Plc
Scarborough House, 29 James Street West
Bath BA1 2BT, England
Phone +44 (0)1225 316013 **Fax** +44 (0)1225 445836
E-mail info@absolutepress.co.uk
Web www.absolutepress.co.uk

A catalogue record of this book is available from the British Library
ISBN 13: 9781472903624
Printed and bound by Tallers Gràfics Soler, Spain

Bloomsbury Publishing Plc
50 Bedford Square, London WC1B 3DP | www.bloomsbury.com

‘The smell of good bread baking,
like the sound of lightly flowing water,
is indescribable in its evocation of
innocence and delight.’

M.F.K. Fisher (1908–1992),
American food and travel writer

1

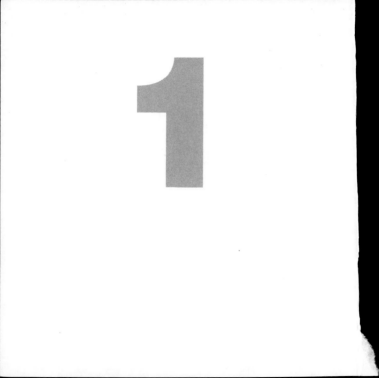

Fresh home-baked bread is one of the most wonderful things you can make. The aroma, the flavour, the texture, the pride in achievement – you'd never get these with a bought loaf.

And **bread is** astonishingly **easy to make,** after a little practice. **With a bread machine, it's even simpler** (and more fool-proof).

2

Buy a bread machine and use it. Sounds crashingly obvious, but a 2010 survey calculated that there are 10 million unused bread machines in the world. So, if you're laying out good money on one, promise yourself to bake bread with it regularly – and that means at least once or twice a week.

3

Get to know your machine.

Before you branch out into more adventurous breads, make yourself familiar with the recipes recommended by the manufacturer in the manual. These will have been chosen to suit the machine and its special features. Each brand of machine will have its own strengths and weaknesses.

4

A bread machine takes up a lot of space.

Even so, it needs to have a permanent position on a worktop or table, where it will always be ready for use. Some people find these objects awkward and heavy to move, so if they get shoved away into a cupboard they may well be ignored and forgotten. Keep your machine visible.

5

Wherever you keep it,

make sure your machine is stable and firm

when it's operating. All four feet should be squarely in contact with a hard surface (not on a cloth). And – if possible – keep it well back from the edge. The kneading process can cause shaking, which could easily make the whole thing move.

6

How big a loaf can you make?

The capacity of the machine's baking pan should be specified in the manual. If you've forgotten it (or lost the manual), simply measure again with water poured from a measuring jug. This will give you the maximum volume for a risen and baked loaf (not for the raw ingredients).

7

Plan ahead. Bread-making takes time

(even with a machine), and there's no way you can produce a loaf on the spur of the moment. The fastest cycle on most machines is at least one, and often two or more hours – and the tastiest bread deserves a lot longer than that to develop its character and texture.

8

Measure out the ingredients precisely. Use the exact amounts specified in the recipes (even if you have evolved your own versions of these). If you overfill the baking pan, the resultant proving and rising could cause the dough to spill out, leading to a nasty sticky mess – or much worse. Cups and spoons are often provided with the machine.

9

Before using your machine for the first time,

season the baking pan (even if it is coated with a non-stick finish). Grease the inside surfaces of the pan with vegetable oil and switch the machine to "bake" for about 10 minutes. Afterwards, wipe off the excess. This process gives the pan extra non-stickiness, and gets rid of any factory taint.

10

Bread's bulkiest ingredient is the flour.

This therefore needs to be measured out even more accurately than everything else. Use a measuring cup, or whatever is recommended in the manual. Spoon in the flour till it reaches the brim. With the cup at eye level, scrape across the top of the cup with a knife.

11

In a bread machine, space is limited.

So remember that **different doughs expand different amounts.** The biggest risers are white-flour doughs, and those which have eggs or fruit in them. Doughs with wholewheat flour, malted whole grains or seeds will rise much less. Adjust your measurement of ingredients to suit the loaf.

12

Measure out the bread ingredients away from the baking pan.

This prevents accidental spillages into the pan, which could lead to overfilling. Only bring the pan over when you're ready to put everything in. Do this well away from the machine itself – again, spillages can get down into the inner workings and get burned by the heating element.

13

Bread ingredients #1: flour.

A bread is only as good as its flour. Anything milled from hard wheat is good (the white flour from this is usually labelled 'strong'). Stoneground wholewheat flour contains the entire kernel, including the bran and wheatgerm, and is best for health and flavour. However, it does make a denser loaf.

14

The gluten in wheatflour gives elasticity to the dough. **For those on a gluten-free diet,** there are plenty of tasty flours to use – spelt, rice, quinoa or gram – but they make rather weak and crumbly bread. You can make your own mixture from those mentioned, but add some xanthum gum to give the loaf a bit of cohesion and spring.

15

Put the ingredients into the baking pan in the right order. This will be given in the machine's manual, or in whatever recipe you're using. Always stick to the order given, or the bread may be spoiled. In general, this means liquids first, flour and other dry ingredients second, and yeast third. However, some machines recommend putting in dry stuff first.

16

Bread ingredients #2: fats.

These are used keep the bread fresh longer, and to enrich the flavour and texture of the bread. As with cakes, the greater the fat content, the more "cakey" the finished texture. Melted butter or refined lard are excellent, but good olive, rapeseed or sunflower oil give an extra tang to the loaf.

17

Try out all possible programmes.

Make all the styles of baking your machine offers, from white or wholemeal loaves to baguettes and rolls, and from fastbake and extra bake to fruit breads and pizzas. Once you know the full range, you can focus on the recipes you like best.

18

Eggs, milk, cream and even yoghurt

can be used along with the other fats in baking. These make a rich dough, and add their own flavours and nutritional elements to the mix. But dairy products also tend to weaken the gluten in the flour, making the bread more fragile and crumbly. Briefly boiling milk before use can counteract this.

19

Bread ingredients #3: yeast.

Without yeast, there would be no bread. Activated by sugar, warmth and water, it ferments, producing carbon dioxide which aerates the dough. For a machine, it's easiest to use yeast in its dried form, and some manufacturers insist on 'fast-action' dried yeast, which contains ascorbic acid.

20

A bread machine in operation can generate a lot of heat.

For safety's sake, place it at least 5cm (2 inches) away from walls and other objects before use, so that air can circulate freely round it. And keep the machine unplugged except when it is in action.

21

Make sure

all ingredients

are at least **at room temperature**

before you start (unless the recipe specifically says otherwise). Yeast simply stops working in the cold. So, if you keep your malted or wholemeal flours in the fridge (as you should, to keep them fresh), take them out in plenty of time.

22

Bread ingredients #4: water.

Liquids spark both the yeast and the gluten in the flour into action, allowing the dough to rise and develop its structure. Water is the most usual liquid to use. Hard (alkaline) water will strengthen the gluten and make a firmer loaf, while soft (acid) water has a softening effect, and makes the yeast work better.

23

Unless the recipe says different, you should

warm the water to blood heat.

This is just the right temperature for the yeast – not too hot and not too cold. Judging it is very simple, with practice. Dip your (clean) finger in the water. If you can't feel anything, it's at blood heat. If you feel warmth or cold, it's not. Adjust by adding cold or hot water.

24

Most bread machines are programmed to monitor temperature and adjust their heating systems to bake at an optimum heat. So they work most efficiently in a room with a steady and moderate temperature. For this reason,

keep the machine away from other sources of heat, such as ovens or radiators.

25

Bread ingredients #5: salt.

Salt does three important jobs. It improves the flavour of the bread; it keeps the loaf fresh for longer; and it slows the action of the yeast. Without salt, the dough would rise too fast and too far before collapsing. But it is vital to use exactly the amount given in the recipe. Any more, and the yeast may not work at all.

26

The **kneading** cycle is the **crucial part of the process.**

This is when the ingredients mix together and turn into dough, and it is vital to have the right consistency. After about 5 minutes of the knead cycle, open the lid and check. If the dough is sticky and wet, add a tablespoon of flour. If it is hard and dry, add a tablespoon of water.

27

Give your loaf a glazed finish.

Rather than fill the machine, switch on and forget about it, you can interrupt the programme (briefly) to add special touches. When the programme is about 10 minutes from baking, open the lid and gently brush on one of the following: whisked egg yolk and water, milk, or olive, sunflower or rapeseed oil.

28

French bread and other low-fat loaves deserve a nice crunchy crust. You can encourage this by lightly spraying or **sprinkling the loaves** a couple of times **with cold water as they bake.** Do this as swiftly as possible. If you leave the lid open for more than a few seconds, heat will escape and the baking process will be spoiled.

29

Once the bread is baked, get it out in the open as soon as possible.

Obviously, the pan will be very hot, so wear oven gloves. Remove the pan, turn it upside down over a worktop (not the floor!) and give it a good shake to loosen it, Carefully remove the loaf and put it onto a wire rack to cool off. This can take an hour or more.

30

Loaf stuck in the pan?

It may be caught on the dough blade. From the underneath, twist the shaft a fraction clockwise. This should free the bread. If not, tap the bottom of the pan gently on a mixing board or other hard surface. As a last resort, slip a plastic spatula down between loaf and pan and clear all round.

31

Once the loaf is out.

Check the dough blade. Is it still in the pan?

Or has it got stuck in the underside of the loaf and been lifted out with it? This is not a rare occurrence. Hoik the blade out tenderly, preferably with a plastic utensil (to avoid damaging the finish).

32

You can also **glaze or top bread after baking.** While it is still hot, brush on melted butter or some thin cream (this will soften the crust a bit). Or sprinkle the top with fine oatmeal, sesame seeds or poppy seeds. Sweet or fruit loaves can be glazed with honey, or with a milk and sugar mixture.

33

Most fresh-baked bread is gobbled up in minutes. But, **if you plan to store the loaf, wait until it is completely cool.** Then put it in a plastic bag to preserve the moisture. If you're freezing the bread, make sure the bag is tightly wrapped round it (with no air pockets) and well sealed. If not, the intense cold dries it out.

34

Use the machine simply as a dough-maker.

By hitting the Dough mode, you get the really hard part done mechanically. Then you can take out the prepared dough and shape it into rolls, buns, muffins, pitta bread, pizza bases and dozens of other things. These are then baked in a conventional oven.

35

Allow the dough to rest and rise for 1 to 2 hours before you shape it. Put it in a greased bowl and cover with cling wrap and a tea towel. Then place the bowl somewhere which is draught-free and warm (but not hot). During this time it should expand by at least half (but remember, white dough will rise more than wholemeal dough).

36

Some bread recipes include **herbs or other vegetables** such as onions or peppers. If these are fresh, they will contain a certain amount of moisture – and this could upset the balance of your mix. So adjust the liquid in your dough accordingly. As an alternative, **use dried** herbs or vegetables.

37

Once the dough has risen once outside the machine, it can be shaped and finished according to the recipe. Do this as quickly as possible, and avoid over-working the dough or it will lose elasticity. Cover again with cling wrap and leave to rise for a second time (no longer than 30 minutes). Meanwhile, heat your oven to 220C.

38

Make sure the oven has reached the correct temperature

before you put in the dough to bake. Then stay alert. Small things like rolls, or thin ones like pizzas, need to be very precisely timed in the oven, or they will get scorched and overcooked (and inedibly hard). Inspect them while they're baking, to check on the colour.

39

Wash the pan out with hot water and a little detergent,

and rinse thoroughly. Use nothing which could damage the seasoning or the non-stick finish. In fact, as a general rule, avoid abrasive cleaners, scouring pads or metal utensils altogether when washing or wiping any part of the machine.

40

If at first you don't succeed, try again.

Machines are designed to make breadmaking a simple and worry-free process. However, things are always likely to go wrong and it's easy to be disheartened by early failures. Keep trying. Analyse your mistakes and learn from them, and you'll very soon be producing consistently delicious bread.

41

Most bread failures have a simple answer. And this often lies in the yeast.

If the bread rises too high and **then collapses in on itself,**

there's probably too much yeast. Measure it more accurately next time. Alternatively, maybe you added too little salt to keep the fermentation under control. Check this too.

42

If the **bread doesn't rise at all, or enough,** there's probably **too little yeast.**

Again, be more careful about your measurements. Other possible causes are: using yeast that's old and useless, putting in too much salt so that it killed off the yeast, or forgetting to put any yeast in at all (it does happen!).

43

Does the top of your loaf collapse when baked in the machine? This may be due to two things. Again, you may be using too much yeast, causing excessive fermentation which gathers at the top of the loaf, and then collapses when heated. Or you could be using too much water, leaving the dough sticky and prone to develop air pockets.

44

If you're

adding sweet ingredients

such as fresh fruit, dried fruit or syrup, you are upping the sugar levels in the dough. This can overwhelm the yeast, and make it work much more slowly. The result is a heavier dough, which doesn't cook all the way through. And the result of that is a soggy centre to the loaf. Adjust the sugar you add at the start.

45

Why are there sometimes big holes in the loaf? Excessive yeast may be the culprit once again, producing too much carbon dioxide, which gathers in large bubbles. On the other hand, you may have used water which was too hot and killed the yeast in patches. Liquids should never be more than blood heat.

46

Sometimes you end up with a loaf that is

sticky or soggy on the outside.

The obvious cause of this problem is: you left it

in the machine too long after baking. Just-baked bread is very hot, and gives out a lot of moisture. With no way of escape, this will condense on the inside of the pan and make the loaf wet. Put it on a wire rack immediately it's done.

47

Loaf like a hockey puck? **If you produce a lump of bread which is hard, dense and dry,** there are several possible answers. Perhaps there was too little yeast. Perhaps there was too little liquid, thus preventing the gluten from stretching and growing. Or perhaps the flour was simply too old and stale to make a springy, bouncy dough.

48

Occasionally, when you open up the machine **you find the bread has stuck to the underside of the lid.** Obviously, you've made too much dough. It may even be impacted and rock hard. Retrieve it and saw off the top if necessary to make it edible. And remember next time to weigh out your ingredients more accurately.

49

Power cuts can happen any time. **Sockets can be accidentally switched off. Act swiftly** to avoid disaster. Most machines have a programme memory of 10 minutes or so. Switch it on again, and it will carry on where it left off. Beyond this, abandon the machine. Remove the dough, finish kneading by hand, leave to rise and bake in the oven.

50

Bread can stay pretty fresh in the **freezer for up to three months.** When you take it out, remember to remove it immediately from the plastic bag and stand it on a rack, so that it thaws out evenly. If you leave it in the bag, the released moisture will condense on the plastic and leave a soggy loaf.

Andrew Langley

Andrew Langley is a knowledgeable food and drink writer. Among his formative influences he lists a season picking grapes in Bordeaux, several years of raising sheep and chickens in Wiltshire and two decades drinking his grandmother's tea. He has written books on a number of Scottish and Irish whisky distilleries and is the editor of the highly regarded anthology of the writings of the legendary Victorian chef Alexis Soyer.

THE LITTLE BOOK OF
BARBECUE
TIPS
ANDREW LANGLEY

THE LITTLE BOOK OF
BEER
TIPS
ANDREW LANGLEY

THE LITTLE BOOK OF
HERB
TIPS
WILLIAM FORTT

THE LITTLE BOOK OF
POKER
TIPS
PETER FRENCH

THE LITTLE BOOK OF
GARDENING
TIPS
WILLIAM FORTT

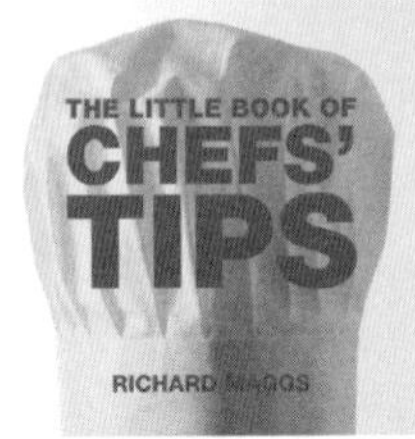
THE LITTLE BOOK OF
CHEFS'
TIPS
RICHARD

THE LITTLE BOOK OF
SPICE
TIPS
ANDREW LANGLEY

THE LITTLE BOOK OF
GOLF
TIPS
PETER FRENCH

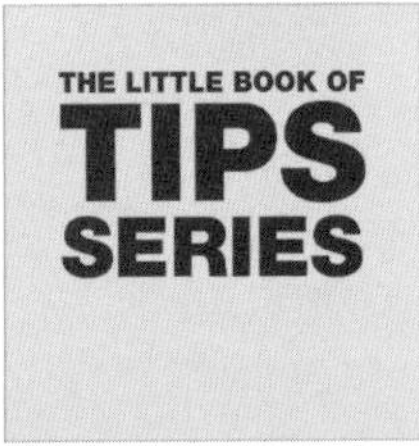
THE LITTLE BOOK OF
TIPS
SERIES

THE LITTLE BOOK OF
CHEESE
TIPS
ANDREW LANGLEY

THE LITTLE BOOK OF
WINE
TIPS
ANDREW LANGLEY
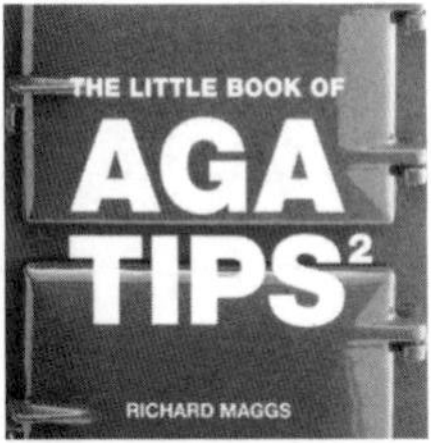
THE LITTLE BOOK OF
AGA
TIPS 2
RICHARD MAGGS

THE LITTLE BOOK OF
COFFEE
TIPS
ANDREW LANGLEY

THE LITTLE BOOK OF
TEA
TIPS
ANDREW LANGLEY

THE LITTLE BOOK OF
AGA
TIPS 3
RICHARD MAGGS

THE LITTLE BOOK OF
AGA
TIPS
RICHARD MAGGS

THE LITTLE BOOK OF
CHRISTMAS
AGA
TIPS
RICHARD MAGGS
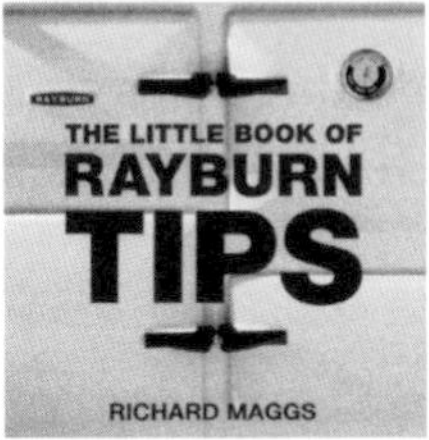
THE LITTLE BOOK OF
RAYBURN
TIPS
RICHARD MAGGS

THE LITTLE BOOK OF
BRIDGE
TIPS
PETER FRENCH

THE LITTLE BOOK OF
CHESS
TIPS
PETER FRENCH

THE LITTLE BOOK OF
FISHING
TIPS
MICK DEVENISH

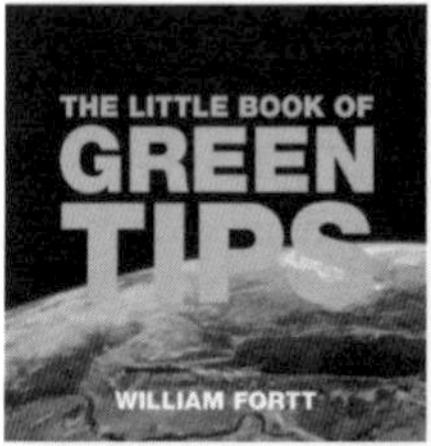
THE LITTLE BOOK OF
GREEN
TIPS
WILLIAM FORTT

THE LITTLE BOOK OF
KITTEN
TIPS
ANDREW LANGLEY

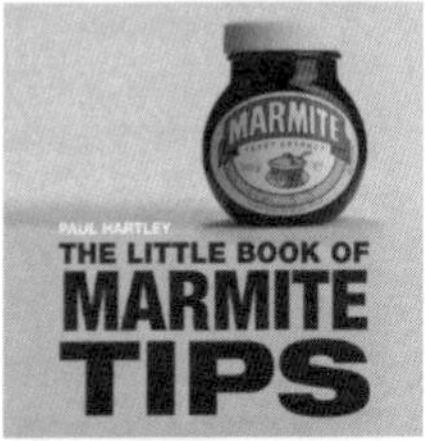
PAUL HARTLEY
THE LITTLE BOOK OF
MARMITE
TIPS

THE LITTLE BOOK OF
PUPPY
TIPS
ANDREW LANGLEY

THE LITTLE BOOK OF
WHISKY
TIPS
ANDREW LANGLEY

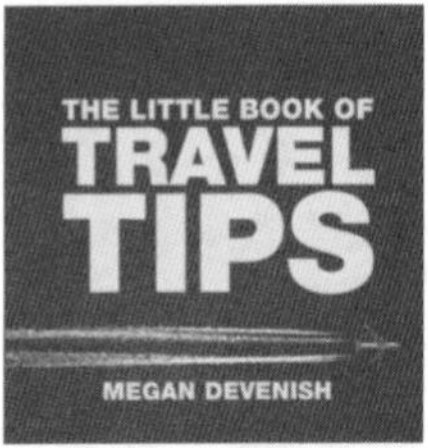
THE LITTLE BOOK OF
TRAVEL
TIPS
MEGAN DEVENISH

Little Books of Tips from Absolute Press

Aga Tips
Aga Tips 2
Aga Tips 3
Allotment Tips
Backgammon Tips
Barbecue Tips
Beer Tips
Bread Tips
Bread Machine Tips
Bridge Tips
Cake Baking Tips
Cake Decorating Tips
Champagne Tips
Cheese Tips
Chefs' Tips
Chess Tips
Chocolate Tips
Christmas Aga Tips
Chutney and Pickle Tips
Cocktail Tips
Coffee Tips
Cupcake Tips
Curry Tips
Fishing Tips
Fly Fishing Tips
Frugal Tips
Gardening Tips
Golf Tips
Green Tips
Grow Your Own Tips
Herb Tips
Houseplant Tips
Ice Cream Tips
Jam Tips
Kitten Tips
Macaroon Tips
Marmite Tips
Olive Oil Tips
Pasta Tips
Poker Tips
Puppy Tips
Rayburn Tips
Slow Cooker Tips
Spice Tips
Tea Tips
Travel Tips
Whisky Tips
Wine Tips
Wok Tips
Vinegar Tips